BURST OF SPEED

Eric,
May the roads rise up to meet you
And the winds be always at your back.
And may you be in heaven
A half-hour before the Devil knows you're dead.
Run fast, my son.

                     —Dad

BURST OF SPEED
5 Proven Techniques to Increase Your Speed

Joe Miller

ICARUS PRESS
South Bend, Indiana
1984

BURST OF SPEED
Copyright © 1984 by Joe Miller

1 2 3 4 5 6 87 86 85 84

Icarus Press, Inc.
P.O. Box 1225
South Bend, Indiana 46624

Photographs by Merle A. Miller;
drawings by Michael Rubino.

Library of Congress Cataloging in Publication Data

Miller, Joe, 1952–
    Burst of speed.

    Includes index.
    1. Running—Training. 2. Physical education and
training. 3. Speed. I. Title.
GV1061.5.M54 1984   796.4'26   84–3802
ISBN 0-89651-705-5
ISBN 0-89651-706-3 (pbk.)

Contents

Introduction

SPEED, QUICKNESS, AND ACCELERATION. THESE ARE QUALI-
ties for which every athlete strives because without a doubt
they are the great "equalizers" of sport. You may not be
strong, you may not have great stamina, and you may not
be the smartest athlete in the world; but if you are quick and
have good overall speed, you may be able to write your
own ticket, for these qualities are indeed the keys to sport
success.

With that in mind, this book is designed for one purpose: to show you how to increase your speed. *Because no
matter how fast you are now, you can become faster, and
no matter how good a player (in any sport) you are now,
you can become better with greater speed.* Do you think being quicker, more explosive, and faster will help your sport
performance? If it will, then this book will help you.

In the chapters that follow you will find a number of
training programs that are designed specifically to increase
your explosiveness off the mark, your acceleration once
underway, and your top running speed. In other words, this
book is designed to make you faster than you've ever been
before, faster than you've ever dreamed possible – fast
enough, in many instances, to make those visions of sport
mastery reality.

1

SPEED: ITS ORIGINS

For many years we thought that speed was innate — that you were either born with it or you weren't; and if you weren't, there wasn't a darn thing you could do about it. However, we now know that that isn't necessarily so. In fact, we have learned that speed can be dramatically increased with proper training. The Russians, probably more than anyone else, have proven this.

In the late sixties, the Soviet Union had a sprinter named Valeri Borzov. Make no mistake about it, Borzov was a fine sprinter. He had his share of international success, but he was by no means the world's best. Up to that point, the most distinguishable thing about Borzov was his durability, for he sprinted very competitively well into his late twenties. And then suddenly Mr. Borzov disappeared from the international track scene. Three years passed, and just as everyone was assuming that Borzov must have been sent packing to Siberia, he reappeared in time for the 1972 Olympic Games. There, he astounded everyone by "blowing away" the world's best sprinters in the 100- and 200-meter runs. So, at the age of 32, Borzov went from a very good sprinter to the best in the world.

How did he do it? For several years, there were all sorts of speculations. Some suggested that Borzov had been taking electrical stimulation treatments; others insited that he was into "blood boosting." Later, however, we learned* that Borzov's sudden acquisition of great speed wasn't due to any of these things, but rather to a training program that was designed specifically to increase running speed. As a result, Borzov went from an "also-ran" to the world's fastest human being, and in the process (although some-

*Apparently, U.S. track coaches visiting the Soviet Union on an exchange program "unearthed" this information. Also, noted U.S. track coach Bill Calloway made note of Borzov's unique training in an article called "Polymetric Training for Greater Speed," *Scholastic Coach* (April 1978):56.

what reluctantly), he and his mentors showed the world that speed was not fixed — that it could be measurably improved, even to a degree that far exceeded our wildest imaginations.

So Borzov and the Russians have shown us the way. The rest is up to you. Will you become as fast as Borzov? Maybe not. But even if you don't, you can become faster than ever before, and regardless of the sport you are in or the level of competition, you can use this added speed to good advantage.

THE SPEED-TRAINING PHILOSOPHY

You will find a number of uniquely different training programs within this book. Philosophically, these programs fall into two main types: those that seek to strengthen and improve the muscular system and those that focus on the brain and the central nervous system. Pursuing speed by seeking to strengthen the muscles certainly isn't anything earthshattering. However, trying to increase your speed by "training" the central nervous system and especially the brain might be. But this is only because sport physiologists have failed to recognize the important role that the brain and central nervous system play in the expression of speed. Speed in every sense of the word is as much a factor of the mind and nervous pathway as it is of the musculature and contractile machinery. Why? Because it's the central nervous system, especially the brain, that places limitations or "inhibitions" on your running speed and quickness.

Physically, we know that modern man has the capability of running the 100-yard dash in less than eight seconds, yet the best he has ever done is 9.1 seconds. In other words, the ability to do better is there, but "something" prevents this from happening.* That "something" happens to be the brain, which keeps us from performing up to our potential for fear that such efforts will make us very vulnerable to injury.

Contrary to popular belief, then, speed is not an element that is totally controlled in the musculature. If anything, it is only "released" in the musculature. The control over that release actually lies in the all-important brain.

Thus, the programs that you will find in this book are dedicated to taking a "holistic" approach to speed training—an approach that strives to strengthen the muscles in order to optimize the force that is "available" to be released, and one that seeks to "train" the brain and central nervous system to release every last drop of strength and power that each of us possesses. With time and effort, the "holistic" approach to speed training will help you to increase your speed dramatically, putting you that much closer to eventual sport mastery.

WHO CAN USE THE PROGRAMS?

Who can benefit from the speed-training programs in this book? Football, baseball, basketball, and soccer players; tennis, racquetball, and lacrosse players; track-and-field performers and even volleyballers—actually, almost any type of athlete can benefit from this book. Because if your sport requires you to move quickly, regardless of whether it is for a distance of three or thirty-three feet, the training techniques described in this book can help you achieve greater speed and greater sport success.

*For further reading in this area, see Yuriy Verhoshansiy, "Depth Training in the Training of Jumpers," *Legkaya Athletika* (September 1967):1618-19.

HOW MUCH SPEED CAN YOU EXPECT TO GAIN?

Of course, to a degree, the amount of speed that you gain depends upon how diligently you train, how close you are to your ultimate potential when you actually start, and how long you stay with the program that you choose. But it has not been unusual to find athletes reducing their forty-yard running speed by .4 to .6 of a second and their 100-yard sprint times by 1 to 1.25 seconds. These are the kinds of reductions that no athlete can afford to dismiss.

In the next section we will be discussing the first means of training to increase your speed: tow training.

1

Tow Training

You won't find any of these "records" in the *Encyclopedia of Sports*, but nevertheless they did occur. Take note:

> At a time when the magic four-minute barrier had not yet been broken, Paavo Nurmi, the fabulous Finn, ran an incredible 3½-minute mile while preparing for the Olympic Games. Afterwards, he remarked on how easy it was.
>
> While engaging in a routine "interval" workout, Australian Alan Lawrence blistered a 220-yard straightaway three full seconds under the existing world record. He could have gone faster, he noted, but he was bothered by a meddlesome blister.
>
> Not long after Lawrence's feat, an unidentified Soviet student rocketed 100 yards in the unheard-of time of eight seconds flat. Upon noting that he had only been in serious training for eight months, his coach said that much faster times were in store for this young man.

Preposterous? Not really. All of these "feats" actually did happen. However, there *is* a catch. Each was performed while the athlete was engaged in a unique training system called *tow training*, a long-known method that is getting a new look from some innovative coaches and other students of the science of running and speed.

What is tow training? As you will discover, it is a very legitimate, if unusual, form of training that is designed to improve an athlete's running speed. In practice, it involves pulling or "towing" an athlete in a strictly controlled manner with a car, light pickup truck, or motorcycle. But with this simple technique, many athletes have been able to make dramatic changes in their running times.

In the next section we will take a look at how tow training came to be practiced and how it works. As the story unfolds, we shall see that this technique is indeed an interesting and genuinely effective training innovation for improving running speed.

HISTORY OF TOW TRAINING

Although we can trace the use of tow training back as far as the 1920s and the era of Nurmi, it is generally agreed that the man who was primarily responsible for bringing it to a level of sophistication was Australian track coach Cecile Hensley.

In the mid–1950s, Hensley worked with sprinters and middle-distance runners and was constantly in search of new ways to make his charges run faster. After exhausting the list of conventional speed-training methods, Hensley came upon the idea of towing athletes behind his car.

As a coach and physiologist, Hensley knew that one of the keys to running speed was stride rate, the number of steps one could take in a given period of time. One of the mechanisms that controls stride rate is the central nervous system. Thus, Hensley believed that tow training might condition the brain or central nervous system to alter the rate of impulses to the muscles and thus induce an accelerated stride rate. A few years later, research studies did show that tow training could increase the athlete's stride rate and running speed. By that time, however, Hensley had already used the tow-training method to help develop several world-class athletes out of a band of formerly less-than-outstanding performers.

That was 1956, and although the sports world hasn't exactly witnessed a tow-training renaissance, the method has been and continues to be used rather extensively in many countries behind the Iron Curtain.*

PHYSIOLOGICAL BASIS OF TOW TRAINING

Sooner or later every athlete reaches a speed "plateau" — a barrier that seems impossible to break through. At this level of speed the neuromotor functions become rigidly fixed so that no matter how hard you try you simply can't run any faster. When this happens, we often assume that the athlete has simply reached his potential and doesn't have the capability to become any faster. However, in most cases this is not true, for there is always a reservoir of strength that one can draw upon to run faster. You have only to know how to break through the speed barrier to get at this strength cache.

*For further information, see: John Tansley, "Glendale's Tow Training for Sprinters," *Journal of Track Technique* 72:2473–75; A. Lawrence, "The Tow Method — Training of the Future," *Track Technique* 1:24–25; and C. M. Sandwick, "Pacing Machine," *Athletic Journal* 47:36–38. Here in the United States, the use of tow training has been rather limited because coaches have somehow got the impression that it was a gimmick and that it had little scientific basis or merit. But that couldn't be any more untrue. Tow training is a legitimate form of training that produces results when used correctly. Fortunately, a few American coaches have had the foresight to stay with the technique after giving it a try and received outstanding results. Not surprisingly, the word has spread, and today we find that the use of tow training is growing steadily. As more and more testimonials come out, the use of tow training could increase tenfold.

This is precisely where tow training comes in. By "overloading" the nervous and muscular systems, tow training makes more of that strength that you actually possess accessible to you. The end results are measurable increases in explosiveness, acceleration, and top running speed. This section will explain exactly how this is accomplished.

To increase running speed, you must do two things: increase the *rate* or frequency of your running stride and increase the *length* of your stride.

The rate at which you stride is extremely important for early speed or the explosive burst that materializes during the first ten to twenty yards of effort. Even the best sprinters, using conventional training methods, seldom exceed 4.4 strides per second. Tow training can boost that rate up to 5.1 strides per second. *Since an increase of .1 of a stride per second may decrease your 100-meter running time by .2 of a second*, then tow training may cut up to 1.4 seconds off your 100-meter running time (.7 strides at .2 seconds per .1 stride).

At forty yards, the critical distance for most sports action, tow training could theoretically decrease your running time by .3 to .4 of a second. So if you are running in the neighborhood of 4.9 for forty yards, you might be able to lower that to 4.5 with tow training.

Of course, these are only projections; however, the results that we have witnessed in the field have been very dramatic. John Tansley, a well-respected coach in Southern California, found that his players decreased their running times by an average of .37 of a second over 100 yards after only six weeks of tow training.

Charles Sandwick tells of a premier high school sprinter who actually reduced his 100-yard running time from 10.5 to 9.9 seconds after only five weeks of concentrated tow training. And in the Soviet Union there have been a number of reports that tell of tow training slashing up to .5 of a second from an athlete's fifty-meter running time.

How much speed will you gain? This is difficult to say. However, we do know that if you increase your stride length (which tow training will do), you will make some gain in speed. Whether it will be as dramatic as these other examples is impossible to say.

During a towing session, it's not unusual to find athletes striding in excess of ten or more feet. This type of striding stretches the quadriceps and hip flexors and increases the range through which the leg can perform.

As opposed to stride rate, which is important for explosive speed, stride length is important for attaining the highest possible running speed and for maintaining that speed over the length of the run. Consequently, the type of athlete who will benefit most from increased stride length is one who plays sports such as soccer, basketball, baseball, lacrosse, and football.

The effect that greater stride length can have on your running speed is quite dramatic. *For every inch you add to your stride you can actually lower your 100-meter sprint time by .1 of a second.* Over time, it's not inconceivable for tow training to pare another .2 to .4 of a second off your measured 100-yard dash time.

PRELIMINARY CONSIDERATIONS

What types of athletes should tow train? Any athlete who thinks that he or she might gain from having greater explosiveness and overall running speed could benefit from tow training. Basketball, football, baseball, soccer, lacrosse, sprinting — if it involves speed and quick movement, this program can help you perform your sport more effectively. Tow training is not restricted to males either. Women can use the program just as safely and with equally good results.

There is an age limit for tow training, however. To be on the safe side, this technique should not be attempted by anyone younger than fourteen years of age; and whenever it is begun, it should be done under strictly controlled and supervised conditions. An upper age limit? Let your good sense guide you there. We all have eventual limits imposed by age; however, if you precondition yourself to such efforts with a great deal of sprinting and flexibility work, you should be able to undertake your training program with safety.

Another important preliminary consideration is *where* to tow train. You should select an area that is very smooth and, if possible, secluded. A seldom-traveled back road is a good bet. At all costs avoid concrete or macadam surfaces; they will chew up your footgear and blister your feet. Outdoor running tracks are not bad options, but they must have a straightaway that is long enough to allow a full 150 yards of acceleration. If your local track can't meet that demand, look elsewhere, for the torque created by running corners at these speeds may injure you.

The footwear you choose will be determined by the surface you run upon. If you opt for a track, you may find that running sneakers or track "flats" will work well. On beaten dirt roads, wear spikes, preferably those that you would use during the performance of your sport. Regardless of the footgear, be sure to wear at least two pairs of socks; tow training has a nasty habit of causing blisters. This is especially true during the initial stage of tow training.

HOW IT'S DONE: TYPE OF VEHICLE, THE TOWING APPARATUS, AND TECHNIQUE

While Nurmi did his tow training by running alongside a freight train and while Hensley (legend has it) used to strap himself to cable cars when he was young, I don't recommend either of these methods. Both are dangerous and inefficient.

So how should you go about tow training? Actually, there are two options. In each, the athlete is towed behind a vehicle that is moving at a predetermined speed. Both the type of vehicle you use and the apparatus you use to support the athlete are important.

The first method involves using a car or "mini" truck to tow the athlete. If you choose this way, you will need to build a horizontal bracket on the back of the car so that the athlete may hold on while he is being towed. Although there are many ways to actually design the towing apparatus, the key is to make it strong enough to support the athlete and to give him stability while running with the aid of the tow.

Several years ago Mark Shuttleworth of Nazareth, Pennsylvania, put together a very feasible tow-training design. Mark's depiction of the "home-built" model appeared in the *Athletic Journal* and has been reproduced below for you. Inquiries about purchasing a towing device can be directed to Mark Shuttleworth, Box 95, R.D. 3, Nazareth, PA 18064.

The base of this apparatus is made of a heavy piece of spring steel, which is lined with rubber and shaped to fit over the upper half of a bumper. The entire apparatus is held in place by a short length of chain that connects a hook at the bottom edge of the bumper with a bolt attached to the tow bar itself. As the diagram indicates, the main portion of the apparatus consists of a four-foot section of 1½" pipe that extends back from the vehicle via a forty-five-degree bend. Two of these primary pieces are attached, and a straight bar runs horizontally between them. This is where the athlete or athletes (two can be safely tow-trained as long as they are paired equitably by speed) hold on during the towing.

The second way that you can tow train is with the use of a motorcycle. Although both methods will induce the desired towing effect, the latter is a little more difficult to perform and slightly more dangerous. If you do choose to go this route, however, you will need to construct a bar or handle that extends back and off to the side of the motor-

SIDE VIEW OF PACING MACHINE

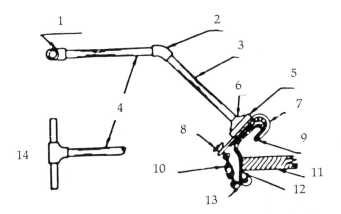

1. Plumbers "T" joint with handle bars
2. 45° elbow
3. 18" section of 1 1/4" pipe
4. 18" section of 1 1/4" pipe
5. Extra metal bracket
6. Flange
7. Bars made of heavy duty spring steel (slips over upper edge of rear bumper)
8. Wing nut
9. Rubber lining
10. Chain links
11. Bracket off bumper
12. Bumper
13. Hook
14. Top view of handle bars

cycle. The athlete will use this as his major source of support during the towing pass.

Undertaking the tow-training workout is fairly straight-forward. Basically, the athlete runs behind the vehicle while being towed in its wake at speeds that slightly exceed those that are possible when running freely. This is done over a precisely measured course and repeated several times during each workout. In this respect, tow training is not unlike other conventional forms of training (tow-training distances, sets, and repetitions will be described in greater detail in the next section of this chapter).

Your running style during tow training should not differ dramatically from your regular running form. However, one thing you must do during tow training is keep your head up. The tendency is to look down at the feet when being towed for speed, but this prevents you from striding out and in the long run may adversely effect the mechanics of your run.

As you run, hold onto the tow bar with one hand (you don't need a death grip; actually a light but firm touch will suffice). Keep your other hand free and pump it up and down with vigor. It's very important for you to do this, for studies have shown us that poor arm pumping is one of the factors that prevents the development of maximum running speed. As you are towed, concentrate but try to remain relaxed. You should feel loose, yet in complete control; and as your stride rate and length increase, so will your speed.

THE TOW-TRAINING PROGRAM

You begin your tow-training program by setting up a measured course. Mark off an area that is 150–175 yards long. Divide this course into three sections, making the first two sections fifty yards each and the final section fifty to seventy-five yards in length. These divisions represent the "speed-buildup," the "maximum-speed," and the "speed-braking" phases, respectively.

The driver who does the towing will pass through each of these sections at a different but measured speed. It's very important that the driving speeds be calibrated as closely as possible to the prescribed course, for much of the success of the program is dependent upon its systematic employment.

Although the "ideal" towing speed has yet to be established, the works of practitioners like Charles Sandwick have given us a glimpse at those towing speeds that have proven useful. The figures on page 16 have been adopted from Sandwick's recommendations. Simply determine your unaided running time for the 100-yard dash, and the table will tell you how fast you should be towed during the various stages of the towing course.

As a rule, athletes should be towed at a speed (during the "maximum-speed" section) that allows them to complete a fifty-yard run one-half second faster than they could do it unaided or to finish a full 100-yard dash from 1.0 to 1.5 faster than their best free-running time for this distance.

SUGGESTED TOWING SPEEDS

Unaided 100-yard dash time (seconds)	First 50 yards (mph)	Second 50 yards (mph)	Final 75 yards (mph)
13.0	15.0	18.5	16.0
12.5	15.5	19.5	17.0
12.0	16.5	20.5	18.0
11.5	17.5	21.5	18.5
11.0	18.5	23.0	20.0
10.5	19.5	24.0	21.0
10.0	20.5	25.5	22.0
9.5	22.0	27.5	25.0
9.0	23.5	29.0	26.0

For the average athlete who runs about an 11.5-second 100-yard dash, then the tow-training course would be set up like this:

Precourse Acceleration	Section One Speed Build-up	Section Two Maximum Speed	Section Three Speed Braking
50 yds.	50 yds.	50 yds.	50–70 yds.
0–15 mps	17.5 mph	21.5 mph	18.5 mph

The numbers that you find in this table are not set in concrete, for as noted, science has yet to determine the "ideal" towing speeds; however, they should be strictly adhered to during the initial stages of tow training to minimize the chances of injury. After a short indoctrination period (approximately two to three weeks), the athlete may experiment with faster towing speeds. However, he should never be towed at a speed that exceeds his best "free"-running fifty-yard dash by more than a second or his best unaided 100 yards by two seconds. There is no added advantage to being towed at extremely fast speeds. Actually, if the towing speed is too great, the "overfast" effect is eliminated because a favorable impression cannot be registered on the central nervous system. Too much speed also subjects the athlete to excessive torque and may result in injury.

During the first two weeks of the program, you should tow-train three times a week and perform three sets of three repeat runs (reps). Rest for three to five minutes between passes and up to eight minutes between sets of three. During the rest period, stretch — especially the hamstrings, quadriceps, and hip flexors.

During the "build-up" and "maximum-speed" phases of the tow, hold on to the towing bar and let the car or bike tow you along. However, during the final fifty yards (slowdown zone) disengage yourself from the tow bar and sprint freely, trying to generate as much speed as you naturally can.

The middle and final phase of each pass are the keys to increasing running speed. The "maximum-speed" zone "overloads" the central nervous system and etches a dynamic tracing along the length of the nervous pathway. The final phase actually etches over this tracing and solidifies it so that the temporary gain in "overspeed" can become a permanent capacity. Together, the two phases of tow training jolt the nervous and muscular systems into a higher plane of contraction efficiency, and greater speed becomes a reality.

During the third and final phase of the towing pass, you may run faster than you ever have in your entire life, and you will be doing it on your own power. True, this is a transitory effect, at least at first. However, with repeated bouts of tow training, this transitory effect can be changed into permanent gain.

Beginning with the third week of tow training, you should increase the distance of the "maximum-speed" zone by ten yards per week and up to 100 yards overall. During this time you may also increase the maximum towing speed. For sets and reps, do 3 x 4 (3 sets of 4 repetitions) and rest as previously suggested. Perform this routine three times a week. This program will serve you well for at least six weeks. At that point you should test out your running speed by being clocked at forty and 100 yards.

If you test out well and have shown good improvement in speed, you might want to stay on this program for about four more weeks. However, if your speed gains are not as substantial as you would have liked, you may want to experiment with different variations of set, rep, and training frequencies. It is okay to do this . . . within reasonable limits. I do suggest, however, that you not exceed four tow-training sessions per week or four sets of such effort per workout. During this period, maximum towing speed also should not exceed an upper limit of 26 mph nor a distance of 100 meters for the "maximum speed" section, unless you are a sub-ten-second sprinter.

Safety and Injuries

Regardless of common assumptions, tow training does not lead to more injuries than other forms of training. As a matter of fact, there have been very few reports of injuries from towing. So, if you've had visions of your hamstrings being torn from the backs of your legs as you go skittering hopelessly along behind a speeding car, forget it.* This type of training is no more likely to hurt you than any other.

Mechanical safety is something else. There is no denying

---

*But this does not mean that you shouldn't practice caution when tow training. You can never be too careful. In particular, you should make sure that the surface you are using has been swept clean so that loose gravel or pebbles won't fly up and hit you. It's also a good idea to work out a series of hand signals with the driver so that you can communicate effectively. And finally it's not a bad idea to wear a mask over your mouth and nose while running. This will keep out any carbon monoxide that may come your way, although that's not likely to be a problem.

that you could hurt yourself if you took a running tumble. Yet even the likelihood of this is very small, and the inclusion of the towing bar really minimizes the chances that this will happen.

ADDITIONAL BENEFITS

In addition to increasing your running speed by altering the frequency and length of your stride, tow training also offers a number of other advantages. First, because it forces your muscles to work through a greater range of motion, it can increase your lower-limb flexibility and make you less susceptible to sport-related injuries in the legs. Because it forces your body to work at higher levels of intensity, tow training also increases your ability to tolerate chemical acidosis and pain. Since it forces the neuromuscular system to synchronize its function at a higher rate of speed, tow training can also improve balance and coordination and accentuate loose but controlled movement under the duress of sport competition. And last, but not least, there is a great psychological advantage to be gained from tow training. Once you experience "overfast" running, you feel quicker even if you actually aren't, and this belief is oftentimes reflected in a newly aggressive style of play.

FUTURE POSSIBILITIES

The evidence can't be denied. Tow training can increase running speed. But how far can it take the speedy athlete? In the future it's not inconceivable to envision man running 8.6 seconds in the 100-yard dash (present world record 9.1) and 4.0 seconds in the forty-yard dash with the use of special speed-building techniques like tow training. But even if you don't come anywhere near these gaudy numbers, you can still make a measurable improvement in your running speed with tow training. Just hook up and go.

2

Hill Training

SPEED. UNADULTERATED AND RAW. THAT'S WHAT EVERY athlete wants, and that's what we're after in this series. The previous section described the practice of tow training and showed how it could be used to improve both quickness and running speed. In this segment we will explore another technique designed to improve speed: hill training.

I'm not sure where hill training originated, but it's pretty clear that the man who popularized it was Percy Cerutty, the legendary track-and-field coach from Australia. In training circles, Cerutty was thought of as something of a maverick, for he was constantly trying out new training devices and techniques that were at odds with the beliefs of the time.

For instance, at a time when every athlete was gorging himself on meats and other proteins, Cerutty had his athletes subsisting on fruits and vegetables. And when no coach "in his right mind" would even let his athletes glance at a barbell, Cerutty had his runners going through vigorous weight-training exercises.

So it shouldn't come as much of a surprise to learn that it was Cerutty who first used hill training to improve running speed. Just as he knew that carbohydrates (fruits and vegetables) and not proteins (meats) were the key to an athlete's success and that weight training could help, not hinder, an athlete's progress, Cerutty had a "gut" feeling that running hills would add significantly to one's speed. And although he never lived to see it happen, research has now shown us that Cerutty's instincts were right; hill training, used in the correct dosage and way, can measurably increase your quickness, explosive power, and overall running speed.

In this segment we will take a long, hard look at hill training to find out exactly what it can do for you and what you have to know to go about doing it correctly.

PHYSIOLOGICAL BASIS OF HILL TRAINING

How does hill training work? In the main, it's designed to "shock" the muscles and central nervous system so that they can become more adept at generating speed. Hill training does this by forcing the muscular and nervous systems to work against heavier loads than they are accustomed to handling. These loads, which are imposed in the form of "overfast" running when one speeds down the hill, force the systems to work "beyond" themselves and result in a temporary gain in speed—which with time and more training can become a permanent addition. In many ways, hill running is not unlike weight training. Weights or hills, the objective is the same: jolt the body, force it to work "beyond" itself, and soon its old capacities will be replaced by superior capabilities.

PRELIMINARY CONSIDERATIONS
Who Can Hill-Train?

If your sport requires you to move quickly for short distances (football, baseball, basketball, tennis, racquetball, etc.) or to move at a high rate of speed for an extended period (soccer, lacrosse, track sprinting, middle distance running), you should benefit from hill training because it will improve your burst (initial 5–15 yards) and your longer-lasting acceleration speed (20–100 yards).

With certain modifications, young athletes too can hill-train. Those youngsters who try it should decrease the recommended frequency, sets, reps, and training distances by one-third. When it is used wisely, hill training can be extremely advantageous to young athletes.* In recent studies conducted in the Soviet Union, it has been shown that hill running may be ideal for young athletes because the optimum time for increasing stride frequency and rate is between ten and twelve years of age. After this age, stride rate can be improved, but not as easily as it can be during the "formative" years.

But no one should start out cold with hill training. It is an extremely taxing technique and should not be taken lightly. Thus, for a period of four to six weeks before you start hill training, you should be doing the following on a regular basis: lifting weights to strengthen the "speed muscles" (quadriceps, hamstrings, hip flexors); running sprints on the flat at least three to four times a week; and stretching daily, especially the speed muscles.

Footgear

No matter where or how you run hills, footwear is important. If you wear poor sneakers or tennis shoes you may not slow yourself down, but you will make yourself very vulnerable to needless injury. Select a good pair of long-distance running shoes, especially those that give you adequate support and an extra cushiony effect.

---

*For more information, see Ozolin and Nikolay, "How to Improve Speed," *Modern Athletics and Coaching* vol. 8, no. 6 (Nov. 1970).

When to Start

The ideal time to start hill training is probably during the off-season of your chosen sport. At that time you should train on the hills just as seriously as you weight-train, stretch, or run to build cardiovascular endurance.

This is not to insinuate, however, that hill training should only be done at this time of the year. Actually it can be started and performed at any time of the year, including during your sport or competitive season (though at this time it should be less strenuous). In fact, performing hill training "in-season" is not at all a bad idea because such efforts will help you sustain the speed that you were able to gain during more intense off-season training.

Selecting the Hill

One obvious (yet very important) preliminary consideration to hill training is to find an appropriate hill. The hill you choose should not be a monster; actually it should be more of a mole hill than a mountain. A hill that rises five to fifteen degrees has proven to be best. Granted that doesn't seem like much; however, the idea is to "stimulate," not overwhelm, the neuromuscular and central nervous systems. The ideal solution would be to find two slopes — one that has a small pitch (about five degrees) and another that is steeper (up to fifteen degrees) — and then to run each on alternate days. The Finns, who have had incredible success with middle-distance runners, do exactly this.

With regard to length, the slope should be 75–100 yards long. Select a relatively smooth surface and be sure to check it for hidden chuckholes so that you won't encounter any nasty surprises along the way.

There are many other recommendations I could make about the hill, but they are not as important. You should not get too hung up on trying to find the "ideal" hill; you could search a lifetime and never do so. The important thing is to find one that is "adequate" and begin.

PERFORMING HILL TRAINING

Although hill training seems simple enough, there's actually more to it than meets the eye. Each hill run consists of three distinct, logically ordered phases: the run up the hill, the run down, and the flat-out sprint at the bottom. To gain a better understanding of how hill training actually works, it might be helpful to explore the basis and the advantages to be gained from each of these particular elements.

The initial segment of hill training, the run up the hill, has two major purposes. First, it strengthens the muscles that generate speed (quadriceps, hamstrings, and hip flexors) so that explosive power or speed "off the mark" can be improved. Second, it builds greater speed stamina — the ability to maintain your fastest running speed even when the muscles are growing weary from the effort.

The run down the hill also has a dual purpose. Here the intent is to smash through the existing speed barrier by "shocking" the central nervous system. This portion of the run is also designed to help you lengthen or stretch out your stride. Studies* have shown that one-tenth of a second can be subtracted from your 100-yard running time for every inch of stride that you add. Hill training may increase your stride length by as much as four to six inches in a very short period.

Thus, if you increase your stride by six inches you could reduce your 100-yard running time by .6 of a second. For a forty-yard dash (the key distance for sport effectiveness) that could mean an improvement of .25 to .3 of a second. So if you have been clocked at 4.9 in the forty-

*For more information see Milan Mikakov and Vernon Cox "Improving Speed by Training on Sloping Surfaces," *Track Technique* 8 (1962):25254–55.

yard dash (a respectable time), you may be able to reduce that time to 4.6 seconds (a super time) with persistent hill running.

The third aspect of hill running is the flat-out sprint at the bottom of the hill. The importance of the sprint at the bottom of the hill cannot be overestimated, for this is the segment that actually determines whether or not there will be a speed gain from the hill-training effort. As I've noted, the run up the hill strengthens your running muscles while the run down the hill establishes a new level of speed. However, this gain in speed is initially very "unstable" and easily erased if it is not immediately reaffirmed. This is where the flat-out run at the bottom of the hill is beneficial, for like the child who writes his name one hundred times to remember it, it reinforces the "temporary" gain in speed precipitated by the downhill run and turns it into a permanent addition.

Scientists are not entirely sure how this is done. Some theorize that the downhill run confuses the central nervous system and makes it more sensitive to messages of higher speed. Others believe that the downhill run establishes a new speed message along the central nervous system and then the flat-out sprint at the bottom etches over it and solidifies it. But regardless of how it works, the important thing is that it *does* work.

On the following page you will find a diagram that summarizes the three major elements of hill training.

TECHNIQUE

The way you run the hill (the form you use) is critical to the success of your program. During the run up the hill, strive for a very high knee lift and a powerful, "bounding" stride. With each step, bounce powerfully off your toes. Avoid short, choppy steps. Use your arms to aid the upward drive by swinging them in unison with your legs.

Coming downhill, the primary objective of your technique should be to stretch out as far as you can. Always extend longer and farther to force the muscles to accept a greater range of motion. Concentrate as you go, for when you hit the bottom you will literally be flying. Here again, arm position is important. Don't hold your arms up like "water wings"; this will only consume extra energy and slow your descent. Carry your arms as you would on the flat. And remember that although the key is to stride out, you should not strain yourself, but rather proceed in a relaxed and confident way.

Uphill Phase   Downhill Phase

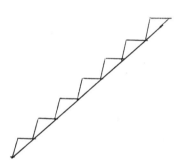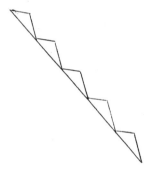

Explosive Speed   Smashes Speed Barrier
Speed Stamina   Lengthens Running Stride

Flat-Out Phase

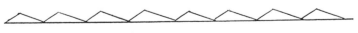

Solidifies New Speed

When you get to the bottom, sprint freely with as much speed as you can generate. Maintain good arm drive and leg lift and strive to sustain the momentum of the downhill run for at least fifty yards.

THE HILL-TRAINING PROGRAM

How should you begin your hill training program? The aforementioned Cerutty had his charges do eight to eleven miles of hill running several times a week; however, you should start with something considerably less. A good benchmark is to begin with the following routine:

3 sets x 3 reps at 50–75 yards

This means that you should run up your chosen hill a set of three back-to-back runs, three times. Between each set of three runs you should rest for a few minutes before beginning the next set. Perform this workout twice a week for the first two weeks.

As noted before, it's important for you to sprint for an extended distance once you hit the flat. At the minimum you should try to sustain your downward speed for fifty yards before slowing to a jog. Then jog an additional twenty-five yards before turning and jogging back (seventy-five yards) to the base of the hill to begin another ascent.

The figure on page 28 depicts the up, down, and flat-out running sequences.

During the third and fourth week you may add a third training session and increase the length of your upward run by ten yards. The first four weeks of hill training will build a firm conditioning base. Thereafter you will be clear to "overload" your speed system more heavily by adding an extra set, rep, and an additional ten yards to your running distance each week, up to the tenth week.

Where should your program go then? Surprisingly, adding even more sets, reps, and distance is not the answer.

This only overfatigues the body. Rather you should strive
to make that which you are doing more intense by carrying
weight on you when you run. A weighted belt or flak jacket
will work extremely well in this regard. Start by adding ten
pounds and then add about 2½ pounds per week up to
twenty-five pounds, or to a level that does not exceed your
own body weight.

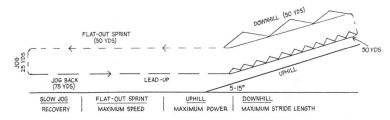

Cerutty was right; hill training *does* make a difference.
Of course, it can't turn a carthorse into a Derby winner or
Humpty Dumpty into Bob Hayes. But whether you're slow,
fast, or somewhere in between, *hill training can and will
help you gain speed.*

3

Weight Training for Speed

ABOUT THIRTY YEARS AGO COACHES WERE VERY HESITANT about letting their athletes lift weights. The general feeling was that such efforts would make athletes tighter, hurt their reactions, and even slow them down.

However, these negative feelings about weight training began to change in the late 1950s when word began to "leak out" that some very prominent athletes were reporting favorable results from weight training.

First, we were told that Heisman trophy winner Billy Cannon was an avid weight trainer. Then we learned that Olympic Decathalon champion Rafer Johnson had trained extensively with weights before his Olympic victories. And soon thereafter it was reported that the world's most celebrated basketball player, the "Big Dipper" himself, Wilt Chamberlain, was heavily into weights.

As the fifties came to a close, such reports became more and more prevalent, and soon a new message began to be passed from athlete to athlete: *the stronger you are, the quicker and faster you can be.* Coaches and athletes began to realize that if you precondition yourself properly, there is no reason why heavy weights will injure you or your performance; in fact, if heavy weights are used correctly they will give you the strength and power you actually *need* to run faster.

Now the eighties have arrived and weight training is here to stay. Medical doctors recommend it, strength coaches make their livelihood from it, and thousands of American citizens use it for any of a dozen reasons. And you, the individual who is interested in improving your running speed, can use weights too. You only need to know how to go about doing it, and this section is designed to give you all the guidance you need.

The weight program that you will find in this section is not a "watered down," all-purpose program that is designed to give you a very general training response. On the contrary, this is a "hard-core" program that is designed with one purpose in mind: to help you become faster. Anything beyond that is incidental, at least for this particular crusade.

Before the actual mechanics of the program are introduced, you might enjoy learning something about the physiological basis of strength gain and how it will help you.

PHYSIOLOGICAL BASIS OF
WEIGHT TRAINING FOR SPEED

Speed is a function of stride rate (SR) times stride length (SL). Stride rate indicates the number of steps that you are able to take per second when running or sprinting. It is a direct reflection of the speed with which you are able to move your limbs. Studies have indicated that the world's fastest sprinters are able to stride about 4.4 times per second.

Biochemically, stride rate is related to the makeup of your muscle fiber (percentage of red and white fibers) and to the efficiency and speed with which nerve impulses are sent from the brain to receptors in the muscles. Empirical evidence has shown that heavy strength training may have a positive bearing on these elements* — on fiber content by forcing more slow-twitch muscle fibers to switch over to fast-twitch and on the nervous system by strengthening the pathways along which the impulses are sent. Both of these effects can give the athlete both greater speed "off the mark" and the acceleration he needs to take advantage of opponents. Tests designed to examine the quickness of Olympic lifters have given us some enlightening information in this regard. It has been shown that these individuals who train exclusively for strength *can actually move more quickly than the fastest sprinters (so much for the theory that weight training will hurt quickness and speed).*

The second element that has a major effect on running speed is stride length. Stride length indicates the distance that you can cover with each running stride. Studies have shown that stride length is not fixed and that it can be positively altered with training. The correlation between stride length and running speed is quite straightforward. If you increase your stride length while maintaining your stride rate (something that can be done with weight training), you should be able to run faster.

The key to stride length lies in the strength that is found in the extensor muscles of the hips, ankles, and legs. When an athlete "strides out," he pushes off with the strength that is generated in these muscles. If they are weak, the force generated during the push-off will be poor and the stride length will be short. However, if these areas are strengthened, much more force can be generated and a longer

*For more information see E. Krucaalak, "Strength Training For Sprinters," *Track Technique* (Mar. 1969):1106; V. Gambetta, *Track and Field Coaching Manual* (New York, Leisure Press, 1981); J. O'Shea, "Effects of Varied, Short Term Weight Training Programs on Improving Performance in the 400 Meter Run," *Research Quarterly* 40 (1969):248–50; J. T. Powell, "Weight Training for Young Track and Field Athletes," *Track Technique* (no. 3).

stride can be produced. So everything else being equal (body weight, stride rate, etc.) you will become faster if you improve your strength because you will then cover more ground with each stride.

Furthermore, although the arms are seldom thought of as being important for running or sprinting speed, strength in these limbs can have a very positive effect on running speed. This is because when you run for speed, arm and leg actions work together in a bilateral way. In other words, as the right arm is being drawn back, the left leg is being thrust forward to cover ground. The action of the arms actually contributes to the power and drive of the striding leg. Thus, if you add to your upper arm strength, you may actually run with greater speed.

OTHER ADVANTAGES OF STRENGTH

Besides the positive effect that strength may have on the biomechanical aspects of speed, strength can also improve your running speed in other ways. For instance, extra strength will help you run with better technique and form and will enable you to sustain your top running speed longer without encountering nearly as much fatigue. This factor of "speed stamina" becomes very important if your sport demands an all-out sprint exceeding sixty to eighty yards.

Further, by strengthening the tendons, ligaments, and joints, added strength will make structural areas less vulnerable to pulls, tears, and other injuries most commonly associated with speed running. And by solidifying the link between the brain and the musculature, strength gain can even add to your reaction speed, enabling you to respond faster and move more quickly once you are underway.

Last but not least, there is the psychological advantage that strength training will give you. When you add strength, you gain self-confidence; you simply *feel* as if you can handle anything that comes your way.

And that is what it is all about — *being totally prepared and knowing that you are.* As you come to grasp this mental attitude, success is almost inevitable.

RECOMMENDATIONS FOR WEIGHT TRAINING

Regardless of whether you are training to climb Mt. Everest or to swim the English Channel, there is a list of do's and don'ts that will help make your efforts more successful. Weight training is no different in this respect, and below you will find those rules by which you must abide when you begin your weight-training program for speed.

- Get on the workout schedule and stick with it religiously. Gaining the type of strength that you need to increase speed necessitates consistency of effort.

- Try to weight-train at the same time each day. Physiologists tell us that this "teaches" your body to gear itself up for the required efforts and results in better preparedness and performance.

- Record your daily workout data in a written log. This will help you become cognizant of where you are at any given moment and will help hold your interest in your program.

- Be sure that you breathe correctly when you weight-train. Many athletes don't. Breathe out whenever you are pushing against the weight and inhale when you are returning the weight to its starting position.

- Try to arrange to have a "spotter" nearby during heavy-lifting workouts just in case you experience some unexpected difficulty and require assistance.

- Perform the weight exercises in the order that they are detailed. They have been placed in this sequence to complement your energy demand.

- Always check your exercise equipment before working out. Make sure that the exercise bar is evenly loaded and the collars are on tight before you begin lifting.

- Dress appropriately for the workout. Wear clothing that fits loosely enough to allow you to bend and stretch in an uninhibited way. Avoid rubber or elastic suits. They make you fatigue more rapidly and may make you more vulnerable to heat exhaustion.

- Wear a leather weight belt when performing those exercises that place a great stress on your lower back.

- Always warm up before beginning your weight training. Eight to ten minutes of jogging in place, stretching, or rope jumping will suffice.

- Strive to add weight to each exercise as often as you can. This "overloads" the muscles and forces them to work beyond their present level. Such efforts inevitably lead to greater strength gain.

- When adding weight to your exercises, do so in increments of 2½ to five pounds.

- Don't become "weight-happy." Concentrate on building strength and power that will make you run faster; don't worry about setting new lifting records.

- Never sacrifice your lifting form by adding too much weight to the bar. Avoid cheating the weight up or pushing it up with body swing or momentum. This may impose an unnatural strain on your muscles and joints.

- Perform your weight training at a measured pace. Rest for only forty-five to sixty seconds between training sets.

- Avoid "testing" your strength or trying for lifting records, unless you are being supervised by someone with expertise in the use of weights.

- Finish each training session with stretching exercises that are directed toward those muscle groups that were most heavily exercised during the weight work-out.

- Don't add extra work to your program by perform-ing more exercises or sets than the program suggests. If you do, you may "overtrain" and actually lose strength and speed rather than add to it. More is not the answer. Putting more effort into that which you do is.

- If you have access to barbells and machines, you might derive better results by using them. They may help you gain more "explosive" power and better strengthen the tendons, ligaments, and joints, pro-viding further protection against injuries.

- Don't make the mistake of ONLY lifting weights. On your "off" days, run, stretch, and perform other speed-training drills (see later chapters). This is the best approach to gaining speed.

- Don't dismiss the importance of nutrition. Be sure that your diet contains enough vitamins and miner-als to promote rapid recovery from training. Don't overload your body with protein foods (meats, eggs, chicken, fish, etc.), since these substances are not needed in nearly the quantities that convention has always dictated.

Finally, an additional word concerning exercise speed. Many athletes believe that you must lift weights with great speed in order to become faster. Thus, when these athletes use heavy weights and find it impossible to lift with speed, they become concerned that they are sacrificing it.

However, this should not be a concern, for the key to gaining speed is not how fast the muscles contract "exter-nally," but how quickly they are forced to work "internally." When you force them to labor under a heavy barbell, all of the internal elements (impulse speed, reactivity, etc.) are working at maximum velocity. So, even if it doesn't appear that it is doing so, lifting heavy weights will dramatically in-crease running and movement speed.

THE WEIGHT-TRAINING PROGRAM

The weight-training program found in this book is designed to increase running speed, quickness, and acceleration and consists of two primary approaches. The first part of the program is designed to give you the "core" strength that you need to develop more running speed. "Core" strength is the type of strength upon which you directly draw when you are making a sprinting effort. It is concentrated in those muscles that are predominately used in your running efforts. The more strength these specific muscles have, the more force that you will be able to apply toward generating speed.

The second portion of the speed weight-training program is designed to perform "transfer" exercises intended to "bridge the gap" between strength and power. Strength and power, contrary to popular belief, are not the same. Strength actually describes the amount of dynamic tension that a muscle is "capable" of generating, while power indicates the actual dynamic force that is "released" when the muscle contracts. In this respect, strength is a measure of "potential," while power is a reflection of what really transpires when the muscle is asked to perform. Needless to say, there can be a marked difference between the amount of strength that one possesses and the actual power that one can release. This factor accounts for the athlete who is prevented from running, jumping, throwing, or hitting with all the speed and velocity that his potential (strength) would lead us to believe that he is capable of.

Misappropriation between strength and power is one of the most frustrating problems in sport. How do we account for it? Although we aren't entirely sure, many sport specialists have theorized that the problem may be due to an impediment within the central nervous system which "inhibits", slows, or otherwise negatively affects the "transfer" of electrical impulses from the brain to the muscle. This condition makes it impossible for an individual to "express" his strength as rapidly or as explosively as he might be capable of. Likewise, this is why he never runs with the speed or quickness that he might be capable of.

Is such a condition unalterable? No, for we have found that the problem can be dealt with most successfully with special weight-training drills that are specifically designed to eliminate the nervous "impediment" that blocks the flow of power. In essence, these drills "bridge the gap" between strength and power and help the athlete generate all the quickness and running speed that he is capable of (more on this in the following chapter).

Mechanics of the Weight Program

This weight-training program is designed to be performed three times a week. Twice a week you will be asked to perform those exercises that make up the main strength-gaining program (core), and once a week you will be advised to perform the "transfer" program.

As you will see, the overall weight plan is divided into a number of training phases. Each phase lasts a given period of time and has a specific objective that differs from that of others. Within this concept there are three basic phases: Foundation, Transition, and Maximum Power.

Phase One (*Foundation*) is designed to be performed for a period of four weeks. The primary purpose of this phase is to "condition" the muscles, tendons, ligaments, and joints so that they will be able to handle the stress of heavy weight training. In an effort to promote more muscle "resiliency" and stamina, you should lift relatively light weights for many repetitions.

Phase Two (*Transition*) is designed to be performed for six weeks. The weight training that you do during this period is designed to act as a bridge between that training which stimulates maximum muscular endurance (Phase One) and that which optimizes strength and power (Phase Three). In addition, this type of training also encourages the development of more lean muscle tissue and gives an individual more dynamic force with which to generate greater speed.

Phase Three (*Maximum Power*) focuses on development of maximum strength and power. Research has shown that maximum muscular endurance can be built by performing an exercise for fifteen to twenty-five repetitions. We've also learned that strength and power can best be built by performing four to six reps per set. This program is designed to accomplish the latter goal. Build as much strength and power as possible. Follow this planned course for six to eight weeks.

As noted, the overall weight-training program is undertaken in three basic parts. The principal idea is to build a firm foundation by beginning with high repetition training and to gradually swing the set and rep scheme around to that which will produce maximum strength and power. At the same time one should also perform the suggested transfer exercises so that the body can be "taught" to use its strength to its fullest degree.

Use the first two weeks of Phase One as a "break-in" period. Do one exercise at a time and do all the necessary work for each one before moving to the next.

Begin with an exercise weight that is not so heavy that you find it impossible to complete the desired number of repetitions, yet not so light that you "fly" right through your efforts.

During the first two weeks of your weight program (Phase One), use the same weight on your exercises. Do not increase the weight until the break-in period is over. During the third week you may begin increasing the exercising weight whenever you find that you are able to reach your target number of reps for two consecutive workouts. When this happens you may increase your exercising weight at the third workout (2½–5 pounds).

At the onset of week five you should alter your program to the set and rep scheme of Phase Two. Continue to per-

form this program on a three-times-a-week basis (strength
and power, twice; transfer, once). During this phase you
may begin using a more advanced training technique that
expedites the strength-gaining process. This technique is
called "pyramiding," and it consists of performing progressively heavier weights with each passing set. For instance, if
your routine called for you to perform three sets of ten reps,
you might end up doing something along these lines:

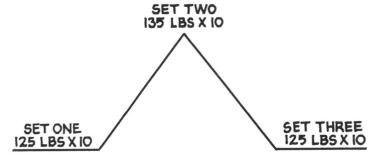

The pyramid is another in the long list of techniques that
are designed to impose a greater "overload" on the muscle so
that it can be strengthened more rapidly. When you use the
"pyramid," you will want to add about ten extra pounds to
the exercise bar for set two. Thereafter you may add 2½–5
pounds to *all* of your sets whenever you find that you can
do the second set for the desired number of reps for *two
consecutive* workouts. Continue to utilize this overall approach for a total of four weeks.

Beginning with the ninth week, you should be performing the work that is marked by the Maximum Strength and
Power Phase. Do this routine three times a week as you did
with others. If you want to make your routine even more
advanced, you can do so by exercising at a given "percentage" of your maximum on different days. The diagram on
the following page depicts how this would be done:

To properly use this training technique, you must "test"
yourself and find out the most weight that you can lift for
five repetitions. This is the weight from which all the train-

ing percentages are derived. For instance, the exercise weight of set one is indicated at 75 percent. Assuming that you found that you could lift 100 pounds for five reps in a particular lift, your exercising weight at this level would be 75 pounds (100 x .75). The figure for set three (102 percent)

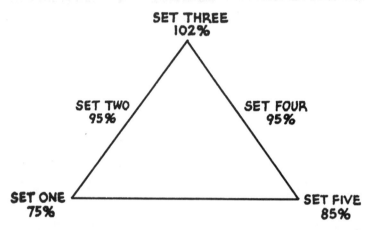

is not a misprint. Actually, here you are being asked to use an exercise weight that is 2 percent above your previous best effort. This effort is asked of you in order to overload and shock the muscular and nervous systems so that more strength can be added. When should you add weight? Do so whenever you find that you can do sets two to four for the desired number of reps (five) for *two consecutive workouts.*

The percentage-training system is not nearly as complicated as it looks, and it is a system that has been shown to be superior in terms of producing strength gain. However, if you do find it difficult to manage, you can apply the "pyramid" concept described in the previous section and you can do so with good returns.

Perform this routine for six to eight weeks and don't be afraid to go heavy. Doing so will increase your strength and power and optimize the climate that is needed to improve running speed. *Remember, the bottom line is that to become faster, you have to be stronger.*

Where does your weight program go from here? After the completion of Phase Three your best bet is to change your program back to the set and rep scheme that you performed in Phase Two. Doing this will give your body a chance to catch up on some much-needed recovery time, while you continue to make more progress.

The return to Phase Two should last about two weeks. Thereafter you may alternately use the programs of Phases Two and Three for as long as they remain productive, which if they are done correctly should be a long time. Over time this approach will work well, because it will keep your body refreshed and you enthused about the weight training that you are doing. The end results will be greater progress and more running speed.

Outlining The Weight Program

Strength & Power Training   2 times per week
Transfer Training (*see next chapter*)   1 time per week
Total Weekly Workouts   3

Do the following exercises for each training routine:

Strength & Power Training
(core)

1. knee-ups
2. kickbacks
3. standing hamstring curl
4. parallel squat
5. bench press
6. arm swing (dumbell)
7. reverse curl
8. front raise
9. power clean
10. calf raise
11. L-sit-up
12. behind-the-neck press
13. hyperextensions

Transfer Training

1. step-ups
2. squat jump
3. scissor jump
4. high-lift running
5. stair jump up
6. triple jumping

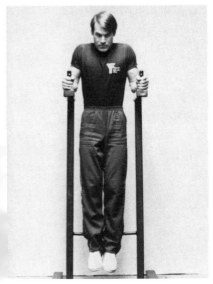 

Knee-Ups

Kickbacks

Place a weighted shoe on your right foot and stand in an upright position about three feet from a wall. Support yourself by placing your hands on the wall at chest height. Keeping your leg locked at the knee, raise your right leg backwards and up, striving for as much height as you can. Pause momentarily at the top position, lower slowly and repeat. **Note:** Try to raise your leg, not swing it.

Standing Hamstring Curl
Place a light iron shoe on each
foot and steady yourself with
light pressure against the wall.
While keeping the hips
stationary, curl your right leg up
behind you — trying to touch the
iron shoe to your buttocks.
Lower and repeat with the other
leg. **Note:** This exercise can also
be efficiently performed lying
down with the iron shoes placed
on a six-foot exercise bar or on a
leg curl machine.

Parallel Squat

Place a moderately heavy barbell on your shoulders and position yourself with your feet about shoulder width apart. Keeping your head and shoulders up, lower yourself slowly until the tops of your thighs are parallel with the floor. Pause and then drive upward with your leg and hips. Control your speed during this exercise. Don't plunge down rapidly or bounce out of the low position. Keep your knees pointing straight ahead during the entire movement.

Bench Press

Lie with your back on an exercise bench and take a barbell from a rack at arm's length directly over your chest. Lower the bar down to your upper chest slowly. Pause at the chest and then drive the bar upward, letting the bar drift back over your nose as you go. Lock out the arms and repeat. Don't bounce the bar off your chest, and keep your hips and lower back flat on the bench at all times.

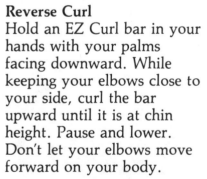

Reverse Curl
Hold an EZ Curl bar in your
hands with your palms
facing downward. While
keeping your elbows close to
your side, curl the bar
upward until it is at chin
height. Pause and lower.
Don't let your elbows move
forward on your body.

Arm Swing
Hold a light dumbbell in each hand with your palms facing upward. Curl the right dumbbell up, thrusting the dumbbell as you go so that your thumbs are facing upward. As you lower the right dumbbell, raise the left dumbbell up in the same way. **Note:** This movement should closely replicate your arm action when you are running; strive for a similar pumping action.

Front Raise *(both pages)*
Hold a light dumbbell in
each hand with your palms
facing backwards. Raise the
right dumbbell up to eye
level, pause, and then lower
and repeat with the left. Try
to lift the weights — not swing
them. Keep your elbows locked
out during this exercise.

Power Clean *(both pages)*
Place a barbell on the floor
and position yourself so that
your feet are directly under
the bar. Bend over and grasp
the bar with your hands
about shoulder width apart.
Bend at the knees and lower
your hips. Keep your head
up and your back flat. To
start the lift, straighten your
legs and raise the bar upward
by pulling with your arms
until it reaches chest height.
Then let the bar roll over in
your hands and catch it at
chest height while dipping
slightly at the knees. **Note:**

Do not bend the arms during
this exercise. Use the arms
singly as hooks and drive
with the hips and legs.

Calf Raise
Place a 2 x 4 on the floor and position yourself so that your toes are on the side of the board. While holding a dumbbell in your hands or a barbell on your shoulders, raise up on your toes, striving for as much height as possible. Pause and lower slowly. **Note:** When holding a dumbbell, do one leg at a time.

L-Sit Up *(right)*
Place your toe under a bench or similar support and lie back. Raise your opposite leg overhead with a slight bend in the knee. Stretch your arms in front of you and curl up at the waist, striving to touch the shoe laces on your upraised leg. Pause and lower, but don't let your shoulders touch the floor in the low position. Try to generate a rocking action during this exercise.

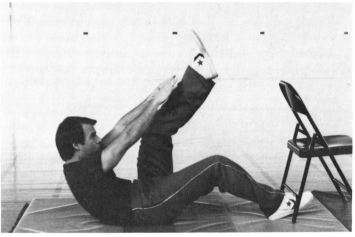

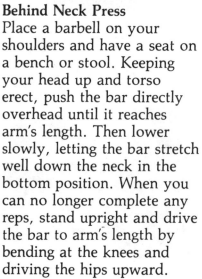

Behind Neck Press
Place a barbell on your shoulders and have a seat on a bench or stool. Keeping your head up and torso erect, push the bar directly overhead until it reaches arm's length. Then lower slowly, letting the bar stretch well down the neck in the bottom position. When you can no longer complete any reps, stand upright and drive the bar to arm's length by bending at the knees and driving the hips upward.

Hyperextensions *(right)*
This exercise can be done on the Universal Machine (shown) or at home. When doing at home, lie crosswise on an exercise bench facing downward. Have someone hold your hips down and place your hands interlaced behind your head. Curl backwards and up as if you are doing a "reverse" sit up. Lower slowly and repeat.

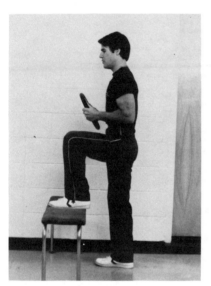 

Step-Ups
Hold a weight plate or heavy
dumbbell in your hands and
stand next to an exercise
bench. Step up with your
right leg and then with your
left so that you are standing
upright on the bench.
Reverse the order when
lowering and repeat with the
opposite leg. Use a bench
18–30" high and push off
hard when stepping up.
Don't be afraid to hold
heavy weights while doing
this exercise.

Scissors Jump
Hold a moderately heavy
barbell on your shoulders
and stagger your feet with
one in front of the other.
While maintaining your torso
in an erect position, quickly
switch your feet front and
back (scissoring). Count one-
half rep with each switch.

Squat Jump *(both pages)*
Position yourself as you would for a regular barbell squat with your feet shoulder width apart and head and shoulders up. Lower yourself slowly to the point where your thighs are parallel with the floor — pause — and then explode upward, striving to jump straight up as high as you can. Land softly and repeat.

High Lift Running
Running in place. Strive to
raise your knees high and to
pump your arms vigorously.
Load on the balls of your
feet with each step.

Stair Jump Up *(righ*
Find a long stairway an
position yourself at the fir:
step with your feet abou
shoulder width apart. Ben
at the knees, lower the hip
and explode upward, strivir
to land three stairs highe
Explode upward during th
exercise. Pause after eac
jump to reset your positic
before jumping. Don't try
jump too many steps
once. Two or three is plent

Triple Jumping *(both pages)*
Here you perform the classic hop, step, and jump. Concentrate on driving with the legs and getting good knee lift during this exercise. This exercise is doubly beneficial because it enhances your coordination as well as speed.

Recommended Training Format & Schedule
(Three Training Sessions Per Week)

	Monday Strength & Power	Wednesday Transfer	Friday Strength & Power
Phase 1	2 x 20	3 x 10	2 x 20
Phase 2	3 x 10*	3 x 15	3 x 10*
Phase 3	Varied*	3 x 20	Varied
Phase 4	3 x 10*	3 x 15	3 x 10*

(a return to Phase Two for recovery and reinforcement)
* Note exceptions

IN-SEASON WEIGHT TRAINING

Should you lift weights during your sport season? You can and actually should, for doing so will prevent you from losing that extra speed that you built during the heavier part of your weight-training program. However, to accommodate the extra energy demand that daily practices and games impose upon you, it is suggested that you limit your in-season weight training to two sessions a week — one session to be devoted to strength and power training and the second to transfer training. In that context, do the following *reduced* programs.

Strength & Power
(once a week)

1.	squat	3x15
2.	bench press	3x15
3.	power clean	3x15
4.	arm swing	3x15
5.	knee-ups	3x25
6.	kickback	3x25
7.	L-sit-up	3x25

Transfer
(once a week)

1.	squat jump	3x25
2.	scissors jump	3x25
3.	run high lift	3x25
4.	stair jump	3x25
5.	triple jump	3x25

RESULTS

Overall, then, it is clear that added strength can have a measurable effect on your running speed. But how much speed will you gain? That's almost impossible to predict because a number of other factors have a bearing on the end result (training intensity, consistency, how close you are to your "end potential," etc.) Still the fact remains that if you weight-train and become stronger, you most certainly will add to your speed. As to what degree, you'll never know until you try.

4

Transfer Training

ONE OF THE CARDINAL RULES OF EXERCISE AND TRAINING IS the principle of "specificity." Specificity tells us that if you want to improve a particular aspect of sport (e.g., running speed) then you must perform some training that develops and strengthens those motor pathways along which the key movements are performed. Experience has shown us that the best ways to do this are by performing exercises that mimic or imitate those skills that we wish to improve, or by doing ones that strengthen those muscles that are called upon most heavily during the skill.

One form of training that does an effective job of this is called transfer training. In this segment, we will learn about transfer training and the effective role that it can play in helping an athlete add to his explosiveness and overall running speed.

Transfer training consists of bounding, hopping, and jumping drills that are a cross between olympic-style weightlifting and agility drills. Although it is concerned with strength, transfer drills actually are *not* designed to *increase* an athlete's strength, but rather to help him *release* that strength that he already possesses by improving the relationship between muscular strength and explosive-reactive power.

Transfer training has been used rather extensively throughout Europe to increase explosiveness and top running speed. There is a great deal of evidence to indicate that Valeri Borzov depended heavily on transfer training in the period preceding his shocking victories in the 100- and 200-meter runs at the '72 Olympic Games in Munich. Just recently, transfer drills have begun to be used in the United States, and the results have been very positive. Football, baseball, basketball, and soccer players have reported improvements of .2 to .5 of a second in their running times. In addition, many athletes have remarked that transfer practice has made them feel more "together" and in better control of their bodies and power. Not surprisingly, the American athletic community is quite excited about the potential value of transfer training.

PHYSIOLOGICAL BASIS OF TRANSFER TRAINING

In the muscles there is a structure called a muscle spindle, which monitors the amount of dynamic strength imposed upon the muscles and works with the nervous and muscular systems to prevent any muscles from being damaged by overstretching.

When the stretch placed upon the muscles becomes too great, the muscle spindle becomes "alarmed" and sends a message to the nervous system to that effect. Through a type of "rebound" action, the message is received at the nervous control center and then quickly "bounced" back to the muscle being subjected to the overstretch. There it stimulates a contraction and shortening of the muscle, thus alleviating it of the dangerous stretch. We call this spindle-nervous-muscle relay our reaction system. One of the principle purposes of transfer training is to strengthen this reactive network.

Although physiologists are quick to point out the "protective" value of this reactive trilogy, they often overlook the fact that this component plays a major role in determining the amount of speed, power, and quickness that the athlete can ultimately generate.

Power is dependent upon two elements: the amount of strength that is found in the muscular apparatus and the speed with which that strength can be released or unloaded. Work with transfer mechanisms has shown us that if reactive ability is poor, the muscles are prevented from releasing strength as fully or as rapidly as they could. As a result, explosiveness, quickness, and overall running speed are diminished or less than what they might be. This condition, which amounts to a disparity between strength and power, has great significance for the athlete, for it is one of the factors that prevents him from running with all the speed and quickness that he may actually be capable of.

By strengthening the reactive complex so that the nervous system and muscular apparatus can work more cohesively, transfer drills eliminate the "gap" between strength and power and help an athlete run (and perform) up to his fullest potential.

WEIGHT TRAINING AND TRANSFER TRAINING

It should be clear, then, that because of this reactive system, one should not train for speed simply by lifting weights. True, there is no other form of exercise that will build more strength than weight training. However, weight training leaves something to be desired because it fails to strengthen the nerve-to-muscle reactive ability. So if you confine your exercise to weight training, you may become very strong, but not very fast. As a matter of fact, you could conceivably develop "world-class" strength and be miserably slow simply because you may have missed out on developing the reactive complex. Transfer training, on the other hand, not only helps you develop strength, but it also improves your ability to effectively use that strength.

Thus, as noted in the previous chapter, transfer training can and should be done in conjunction with regular weight training, for no two activities complement each other any better than these two. Weight training adds to your level of strength, and transfer training insures that you will be able to make full use of that strength which you do add. Together they will help you become faster than you have ever been before.

What type of weight training should you do? Although you should be on a well-rounded program that is designed to strengthen the entire body, you should take special care to strengthen the hips, lower back, and legs, for these are the areas that are most heavily used during transfer training, and, for that matter, while you are running for speed.

When weight training and transfer drills are combined, try to do them on separate days. If this is impossible, divide your transfer workout over several days rather than just one.

PRECONDITIONING

Because transfer drills are more stressful than other more conventional forms of training, it is advisable to precondition the body with eight to ten weeks of weight training before undertaking them. These efforts will give you the foundation that you need to prevent injuries and to reap the full benefit of the transfer-training effect.

Furthermore, because of the "braking" stresses placed on tendons, ligaments, and joints, these drills may not be good for athletes younger than fourteen years of age. In this respect, the Russians believe that no athlete should undertake transfer training until they are capable of performing a barbell squat with twice their own body weight. This should give you some idea of the potential stress of transfer training.

In addition to pretransfer weight training, you should also perform jumping drills between benches while holding light weights. Begin your actual transfer training conservatively. Don't overstretch your muscles with overexaggerated bounds and restrict your jumping height to a maximum of twelve inches during the first two weeks of training.

EQUIPMENT AND SAFETY

The ideal place to perform transfer drills is in a matted area such as a wrestling room or where a number of elastic or foam mats have been placed end to end. If you must train outside, try to find an area with soft grass or sand. For footgear, wear sneakers that have a cushiony sole and provide good support. Insert heel cups into the sneakers to reduce the stress imposed upon the feet during ground impact.

THE TRANSFER-TRAINING PROGRAM

The transfer program is divided up into two groups of exercises. Group One exercises have been shown to improve explosive speed (initial fifteen yards of running) and high speed acceleration once underway. Group Two exercises will help increase your top running speed and your ability to maintain running speed.

Group One	Group Two
1. Speed Chops	1. Power Bounds
2. Quick Hops	2. Box – Ground – Jumps
3. Depth Jumps	3. Box – Ground – Hurdles

Start out by doing both groups of exercises twice a week for four weeks. During the fifth week of training you may add a third weekly training session.

Use the following set, rep, and distance format when undertaking this program:

Speed Chops	2x30 yards; increase distance by five yards per week up to a maximum of 75 yards; add one rep every two weeks up to a maximum of five reps.
Quick Hops	6x40 yards; increase distance by 5 yards a week up to a maximum of 100 yards; add one rep every two weeks up to a maximum of five. (two reps each for double leg; left leg; and right leg only)
Depth Jumps	2x8 at 30 inches in height; add one rep per week up to a maximum of twelve; add one set every third week up to a maximum of six. 2x8 at 44 inches in height; add one rep per week up to a maximum of twelve; add one set every third week up to a maximum of six
Power Bounds	6x40 yards; increase the distance by 5 yards per week; add one rep every third week
Box – Ground – Jumps	2x8 at 30 inches to 44 inches 2x8 at 44 inches to 30 inches add one rep to each exercise a week up to a maximum of twelve; add one set to each up to five
Box – Hurdle – Jumps	2x8 at 30 inches 2x8 at 44 inches add one rep per week up to a maximum of twelve and one set up to a maximum of five

Perform one exercise at a time, resting about forty-five to sixty seconds between reps and up to three minutes between exercises. Stretch before and after to minimize soreness and fatigue.

EXERCISE PERFORMANCE

Speed Chops

This is a simple drill designed to improve your mechanical running form. It involves running in place while moving slowly forward with quick, chopping steps. Lift your knees high and land on the balls of your feet. Move straight ahead and keep the toes pointed forward at all times. Land lightly on your feet and emphasize a "pitter-patter" type foot action with maximum speed. Pump the arms vigorously in unison with movement of the feet.

Quick Hops

The emphasis in this exercise is on forward speed. Make short, powerful double and single leg hops with a low trajectory. Exaggerate the leg movement by trying to touch both heels to the buttocks when you hop. Swing the arms in unison, using double and single arm swings. Think "speed" in this exercise (children call this the "bunny hop").

Depth Jumps

Begin by standing on a box built to the appropriate height (see program). Drop off the side of the box and land resiliently on the balls of the feet. Don't allow your legs to bend lower than 90° at the point of ground impact. Upon landing, immediately spring up into a "rebound" jump, striving for as much height and power as possible. Keep your torso erect and your pelvis tilted upward during the landing and takeoff. Hang an object over the "rebound" area and strive to jump up and touch this object. Over time, increase the height of this object. Perform these jumps in a "matted" area such as a wrestling room. Wear heel cups to absorb ground impact.

The heights from which you jump are very significant. Verhoshanski has shown that jumps made from thirty inches were ideal for developing the nerve-to-muscle "reactive" ability and explosive strength, while those performed at forty-four inches were determined to be best for improving both dynamic strength and one's top rate of running speed.

Power Bounds

This exercise consists of performing an elongated running stride in which you strive to push off with maximum power and then "float" through the air as far as possible. Landing should be made lightly and the feet should "give way" so that there is a very obvious "bouncing" effect. This is the type of stride that you might make if you were forced to jump over several consecutive puddles while holding an arm full of books. Be sure to use a high knee and thigh lift when swinging the leading leg out. Strive for length and smooth transfer from one foot to the other.

Box — Ground — Jumps

This exercise is very similar to depth jumping and is performed the same way with one slight modification. Upon landing you must immediately try to jump back up onto a second box that has been positioned in front of you. The positioning of this box can vary depending upon the training effect that you are trying to produce. Setting the box at a height of thirty inches will develop nerve-muscle reactive ability and explosive speed, while forty-four inches will best develop acceleration and overall running speed. Alternating between the two will develop all aspects of speed.

Box — Ground — Hurdles

For this exercise you position yourself on top of a box and drop off the side much as you would for depth jumping. However, rather than jumping "upward" upon landing, you should instead jump straight forward over a series of hurdles set at specific distances. The type of hurdle jump that you perform will ultimately determine the speed-training effect. To develop explosive speed you should set the hurdles close together and strive to jump over them as quickly as possible. Alternate double and single leg jumping. To build long-range speed (30 to 100 yards) set the hurdles farther apart and emphasize longer bounds with explosive takeoffs.

Speed Chops   Quick Hops

Depth Jumps

Power Bounds

Box–Ground–Box Jumps

Box–Hurdle Jumps

*(counterclockwise from
upper left)*

RECOMMENDATIONS

- Build a firm strength base with weight-training exercises before undertaking Transfer Training.

- Never do Transfer Drills on two consecutive days, unless you divide up the workload (i.e., Mon.: Group One; Tues.: Group Two).

- Perform all Transfer Drills with maximum speed, explosiveness, and power.

- Always perform Group One exercises BEFORE Group Two; never switch the sequence.

- If you are performing additional speed work, do Group One exercises BEFORE this work and Group Two exercises AFTER.

- Perform your Transfer Drills on different days than your regular weight training.

- After a session of intense Transfer Training, follow up with a running workout that stresses endurance (slower, longer duration).

- Do the brunt of your Transfer Training during your sport off-season.

- Increase the frequency and volume of Transfer Training in the immediate period (four weeks) after the completion of a heavy strength-training period.

- When using Transfer Training during the sport season (this can be done with safety and good results) limit your use to ONE workout a week and do only 60 percent (volume) of the Transfer work that you initially began with.

OVERLOADING

Weight training has shown us that you must constantly strive to "overload" the muscles to become stronger. This is also true with transfer training. To become quicker and faster you must strive to overload or "shock" the reactive system with greater demands. This can be done in two ways. For jumping drills (off a box) you can overload by increasing the height of the takeoff (up to a sensible level). Do this over time, slowly, one inch at a time. However, you should never increase the takeoff height to the point where the impact might overstress or injure you; fifty inches is the maximum allowable height for box jumps. Besides, beyond this height more dynamic strength than reactive ability is built.

For quick hops and repetitive bounding, you can "shock" the reactive system by attaching a small amount of weight to your waist (with a weighted belt). This will force the reactive network to work against even greater resistance and may optimize strength, speed, and power.

JUMPING, BOUNDING, AND SPEED: CONCLUDING REMARKS ON TRANSFER TRAINING

Many athletes have difficulty understanding how "jumping" or "bounding" for distance can possibly have a positive effect on running speed. If you are having similar doubts, you may be thinking of speed solely in mechanical terms.

It is important to emphasize that transfer training is not targeted at the mechanical, but at the neurological (spindle-nervous-muscle) aspect of speed development. In other words, transfer drills are not so much designed to increase your dynamic strength or even your ability to jump or bound as they are to "shock" the nerve-muscle reactive apparatus into more cohesive action.

To date, American physiologists have scoffed at the idea that the neurological aspect of speed expression could be trained and improved, yet European specialists have been designing training programs for this very purpose for years. If nothing else is to be gained from this report, *it is impor-*

tant for athletes, coaches, and sport scientists to understand that the possibility of developing the neurological aspect of strength and speed expression is very real and much greater than we have ever believed.

To this end, I have my own ideas as to exactly why transfer training is so beneficial. I believe that transfer training possibly strengthens and deepens the channels along which the cerebral cortex sends its contractile messages, maximizes the size of the electrical volley that is jettisoned from the upper thought processes, and perhaps even increases the efficiency with which the muscle can pick up commands and turn them into power and speed.

These are, of course, only personal suppositions that as yet cannot be verified by clinical data. However, until more in-depth analysis is conducted upon the neurological system, these speculations may in part explain the effectiveness of the transfer technique. The key point to remember is that transfer training does not simply strike at the mechanical (muscular) level, but goes deeply into the body to strengthen the neurology that is critical to the development of strength and speed.

5

Stretching

OF ALL THE ELEMENTS THAT GO INTO THE PREPARATION FOR sport, the one most of us take least seriously is stretching. "I'll do it tomorrow," we say. But alas, tomorrow never comes, and that is a shame because there are many fantastic benefits to be gained from consistent stretching.

For instance, stretching can help you avoid many needless injuries by making your muscles, ligaments, and tendons more pliable and resistant to the strain of athletic participation. In this way, stretching can help alleviate much of the soreness of early-season training and even help you recover more quickly from one workout to the next. Further, by letting you try more advanced techniques, stretching can enhance your overall ability. But most importantly, at least in the context of this report, *it has been shown that stretching can help you gain running speed by lengthening your stride, allowing you to generate more power over a greater time period.* For instance, in a study conducted over an eight-week period, it was shown that stretching could cut running time by four-tenths of a second.*

*For more information, see G. B. Dintiman, "The Effects of Various Training Programs On Running Speed." *Research Quarterly* 35 (1964):456–63; B. Ehrart, "Thirty Russian Flexibility Exercises For Hurdlers," *Athletic Journal* (Mar. 1976):38–39; G.B. Dintiman, *What Research Tells the Coach about Sprinting* (AAHPERS Publications, 1974), 15.

PHYSIOLOGICAL BASIS

Physiologists believe that stretching works to improve running speed by decreasing internal resistance, increasing stride length, promoting more efficient movement through a range of motion, and helping the athlete perform longer and more intensely without expending as much energy. Each of these factors is discussed below.

Internal Resistance

Every time you run, especially with quickness and speed, some of your body's strength must be used to overcome the internal resistance that is stored in the muscles. Although this resistance actually exists to protect you from injuries, it is detrimental to speed because it prevents you from applying your full power when running. As a result, you never move quite as quickly as you might if it did not exist. By opening up internal pathways in and around your muscles, stretching helps cut down on some of this resistance and frees the muscles up to contract more forcefully. The end results are more power and greater running speed.

Stride Length

Along with stride rate, stride length is one of the key factors that ultimately determine running speed. Stride length, of course, indicates the "ground" that you can cover over the length of a single stride. If everything else (stride rate, reactive ability, running mechanics) is equal, a simple increase in stride length will result in a betterment in your running speed.

By allowing the legs to stretch out and to work through a greater range of motion, flexibility training can have a very positive effect on stride length and ultimately on running speed itself.

Movement Efficiency

There are two types of flexibility: static and dynamic. Static flexibility indicates the degree to which a muscle can flex or extend, while dynamic flexibility indicates how easily the joint can be moved through its productive range of motion. Although both of these forms of flexibility are important, athletes have an especially critical need for dynamic flexibility because it allows them to express their *fullest* strength, power, and speed — their *maximum running efficiency*. Dynamic flexibility can be improved by combining specific stretching with the practice of one's sport skill.

Energy Conservation

Because of the internal inertia that lies in the muscles, the faster you run, the more strength you have to apply to sustain your speed. So to run with maximum speed, you have to apply your strength productively. If you are inflexible, too much of your strength is consumed by overcoming internal resistance to allow you to run with the greatest possible speed. To perform up to your fullest speed potential, you must loosen up. Stretching is the logical solution.

KEY MUSCLES

The areas that you must concern yourself with if you are stretching to improve running speed are the ankles, the hips, and (surprisingly enough) the shoulders.

Flexibility is needed in the ankles to maximize the drive during the push-off phase of striding and to help you handle the harsh impact of running strides. The hips also need to be flexible to contribute to the thrust imparted during sprinting and to allow greater knee lift and power development. Shoulder flexibility is necessary to take advantage of the power that develops from the rhythmical swinging of the arms. The greater the range of motion here, the more power can be developed and transferred to the legs.

Although flexibility in all three of these areas will help all athletes in their pursuit of greater running speed, those who may derive particular benefit are those individuals with short legs and inflexible joints.

FLEXIBILITY: BASIC INFORMATION

How to Stretch

1. Start by stretching slowly to a point where you feel mild discomfort. Hold that point for about twenty seconds, then relax and return to the starting position.
2. Perform a second stretch to a point that is slightly beyond that which you stretched to with your first effort; hold this stretched position for thirty seconds.
3. The second stretch should be more intense; however, it should not be painful.
4. During the second stretch, you should feel the tension subside somewhat; if it does not, you may be overstretching: back off slightly.
5. Perform all stretches slowly and easily.
6. Avoid quick or jerky movements; perform everything in a controlled fashion.
7. Don't bounce or try to assume a position that you are not ready for.
8. Tune into your muscles; try to "feel" the lengthening of the muscles.

When to Stretch

When should you stretch? If you are trying to gain maximum benefit, probably the ideal times to stretch are immediately *before* and *after* your other structured speed training (i.e., weight training, hill running, tow training). Stretching performed before your regular workout will loosen the muscles and prep them for the training they are about to engage in. Performed after the speed-training workout, stretching helps remove exercise waste products that tend to make you sore and that slow recovery time.

These are probably the best times to stretch, but not the *only* times. Actually you can do so whenever you have the time. Like any other form of structured training, however, it is advisable to set aside a specific time of the day for your flexibility work. Doing this will help you maintain consistency and will lead to more rapid progress.

Clothing and Environment

The clothing that you wear when you stretch should be very similar to that which you lift weights in — lightweight, comfortable, and loose-fitting enough to allow you to move into and out of stretched positions in an unencumbered way.

Do your stretching in a warm area. In this regard you do not have to turn the thermostat up to 90°, but something like a cold cellar floor is quite the opposite to what you need to stretch properly. (Cold tends to cause the muscles to constrict and to fight your efforts to lengthen them.)

THE STRETCHING PROGRAM

There are a total of fourteen stretches in this routine. Some exercises have two parts; on these do each part once. Do all other exercises twice (two reps), alternating leg positions and stretching motions for exercises involving two possible positions or motions. If you do all your stretches in one session, this routine will take approximately twenty-five to twenty-eight minutes. If you wish, you may divide the routine in half and do one portion of it before your regular training workout (i.e., weights, hill runs) and the second part after. Perform the entire routine at least five times a week — seven would be even better.

Hurdler's Hip Flexor Stretch
While bracing your hands against a wall, alternately bring your knees up and forward; hold for six to eight seconds at that point beyond parallel.

Front Splitters (I)
Move one leg forward until the knee of the forward leg is directly over the ankle. Rest the other knee on the floor. Lower the front of your hip downward to create a stretch; you should feel a pulling sensation in the hips, groin, and hamstrings.

Groin Stretcher
Squat down with your feet flat and toes pointed out slightly; heels should be four to twelve inches apart; keep knees to the outside of the shoulders; this stretches the knees, lower legs, back, ankles, achilles tendon, and groin.

Front Splitters (II)
Assume a position similar to Front Splitters (I); however, instead of lowering the hips downward, lower the torso and head; keep the hips in a stationary position.

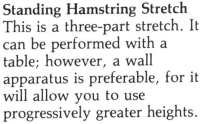

Standing Hamstring Stretch
This is a three-part stretch. It can be performed with a table; however, a wall apparatus is preferable, for it will allow you to use progressively greater heights.

(Part One)
Place your heel on a table or rack at waist height; keep the extended leg straight; bend the lower leg slightly at the knee with your foot pointing forward; extend your hands toward your feet and slowly bend forward at the waist;

hold the point of discomfort, then relax and repeat; you should feel this in the back of the leg.

(Part Two)
Now place your leg on a higher table (or if using a wall rack on a higher rung) bend your forward extended leg slightly (about one inch); you should be on the toes of your trailing leg; from this position bend at the waist and try to draw the chest and head down to the raised leg; stretch; hold for twenty seconds.

(Part Three)
Assume a position much
closer to the table or wall;
place your heel on the
support with a bended knee
so that the thigh is close to
your chest; raise up on the
toes of the trailing leg and
draw your hips inward so
that your thigh comes into
contact with your chest; hold
for twenty seconds; relax;
repeat.

Chicken Wing
Lean against a wall with one
hand and reach behind you
and grasp your ankle with
the other; (left hand-right
ankle) gently draw the foot
towards your buttocks and
hold when you feel a good
stretch in the quadriceps and
knee areas; don't jerk the leg
or try to apply too much
force.

Head To Knees
Assume a seated position
with the legs straddling to
the side; keeping the legs
straight and in contact with
the ground, extend both
arms out toward your left
ankle; grasp the ankle and
slowly draw the chest down
toward the left thigh; hold
that point where you begin
to feel discomfort for twenty
seconds; relax and restretch
to a point slightly beyond.

Chest To Ground
Assume the same starting
position as above; while
keeping the legs straight and
in contact, place your hands
on the floor in front of you
by bending at the waist;
slowly "walk" your fingers
forward until you reach a
point of discomfort in your
lower back and hips; hold
that point; relax and "walk"
your hands out again; keep
your back straight when
performing this exercise.

Pike *(Chest To Knees)*
Assume a seated position as
shown; if you are extremely
tight in the lower back take a
towel and wrap it around the
bottom of your feet; while
keeping your legs extended
straight ahead and in contact
with the ground, slowly
lower your torso so that
your head moves toward
your toes; do this by inching
your way down the towel;
move forward to a point of
mild discomfort; hold for
twenty seconds; relax; repeat
for thirty seconds more; keep
the back flat and don't
bounce.

Wall Stretch

Lean against a wall with the feet in a staggered stance — right foot about eighteen inches away and the trailing leg about three and one-half feet from the wall; place the foot closest to the wall in a bent position and keep the trailing leg locked; with the heel of your trailing leg flat on the floor, slowly move the hips forward; stretch to the point of discomfort; hold for twenty seconds; relax and repeat; you should feel a stretch in the calf and achilles tendon of the trailing leg.

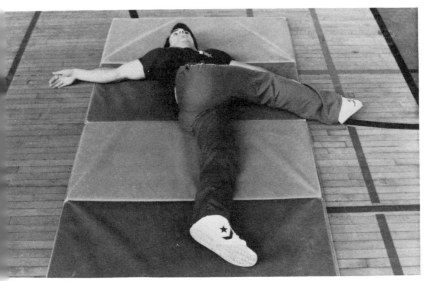

Side-to-Side Stretch (left)

Place one leg on a support of waist height; turn the foot so that the toes are pointing outward; keep your torso pointing straight ahead; place your hands on your waist and bend your left elbow to your left knee; you should feel a lot of stretch on the inside of your raised leg; hold at the point of discomfort and repeat.

Foot-to-Hand Stretch

Lie flat on your back, legs together, arms extended to your sides with the palms down; bring your right leg over and touch your left hand; as you do, keep the other hand, arm, leg in contact with the floor; hold the right toe as close to the left hand as possible for maximum stretch in the hamstring, groin, and hip areas.

Super Groin Stretch
Position yourself about six inches away from a wall with your lower back flat and your legs bent overhead with the heels together and against the wall; from this position slowly spread your thighs apart while keeping the heels together and against the wall. This creates a vigorous stretch on the groin so stretch within your limits; to increase the stretch, place your hands on the inside of your thighs and press lightly downward.

Look Back Stretch
This stretch is a continuation of the previous exercise; when you reach the position of maximum stretch with hands outstretched in front, take the hand that matches the outstretched leg (right hand—right leg) and place it out to the side for balance; then twist slightly at the hips and look over your right shoulder; hold the point of maximum stretch and then relax, this will stretch your upper and lower back, hamstrings, and muscles along the spine.

Hurdlers Two Part Stretch
(left)
Assume a seated position with one leg extended forward and the other leg tucked underneath with the heel just to the outside of the hip; try to keep the foot of the bent leg pointed backwards rather than flared to the side; slowly bend forward at the waist and stretch the hands toward the feet; keep the outstretched leg upright with the foot flexed backwards; strive to draw your chest down to your thigh; don't bounce.

RESULTS

How quickly can you improve your flexibility? Of all of
the elements that form the basis of athletic effort (strength,
power, endurance, etc.), flexibility can probably be improved most rapidly. In this respect, some studies have
shown that it is possible to make significant changes in flexibility in as little as two to three weeks.*

*For more information see H. A. DeVries, *Physiology Of
Exercise in Physical Education and Athletics* (New York: William
C. Brown Co., 1966).

6

Final Thoughts

IF YOU'VE GOT TO THIS POINT, YOU'RE PROBABLY PRETTY EX-
cited about the possibility of using these programs to increase
your quickness and speed. But you also probably have a lot
of questions that need to be answered before you are ready
to commit yourself to doing these programs: How do I get
involved? How much time and effort do I have to put into
training for speed? And, of course, what kinds of results
can I expect?

This chapter has been written to address those types of
questions and concerns and even reservations that you may
have about the program(s). So if you've had a question
lingering in your mind or something that you read along the
way was unclear, read on. This final chapter may help
everything fall into place for you.

First, **which programs should you use?** Unless you can
identify a specific weakness (i.e., lack of strength, poor flexibility) that you think is holding you back from running
faster, you should use *all* the outlined programs, but not all
at once. If you were to do that, it not only would take up all
your free time but you would be so overworked that you
would end up losing speed rather than gaining it.

The way to incorporate all of the programs into your
training is by using the cycling concept that was outlined in

the section on weight training. With cycling, the basic idea is to concentrate on one (sometimes two) programs at a time for four to eight weeks and then to switch to another program or form of training that is slightly different. This concept produces maximum results because it allows you to devote all your energy to one form of training at a time. Because it allows you to use all of the programs, over time it will also help you eliminate weaknesses that you have not been able to readily identify.

The cycling plan is an extremely effective way to train during the off-season if you are an athlete. For example if you were into baseball here is how you might use the period between the end of one season and the start of the next to increase your quickness and running speed.

Month One	Weight Training & Stretching
Month Two	Weight Training & Stretching
Month Three	Weight Training; Stretch; & Transfer Training
Month Four	Weight Training; Stretch; & Tow Training
Month Five	Weight Training; Stretch; & Downhill Running
Month Six	Transfer Training; Stretch; & Downhill Running
Month Seven	New Season Begins

As you can see different programs are combined over the course of the off season. At the beginning of the off-season, it's imperative to build a solid muscular foundation, so weight training is emphasized. As the off-season progresses, other programs (transfer training, tow training, etc.) are incorporated to teach you how to use the strength you've gained to generate greater speed. Over the entire period, stretching is included to help your body tolerate the strains of training and to keep you from injuring yourself.

How should you use the cycling program? Although the example above was designed for baseball players, it is useful for all types of sports and can be adapted to fulfill the off-season speed-seeking needs of any type of athlete. So regardless of the sport you're in, you can use the above example as a model for your own off-season program.

How much effort will you have to put into these programs to make them work for you? The fact is you won't make any progress without exerting yourself, but that does not mean that you have to kill yourself or to dedicate your entire life to this type of training to make some gains. Train hard and consistently but don't overtrain, and you will get the results you are after. Your motto should be to push yourself to the same degree that you would while practicing your own sport. Not anything less — nor anything more.

What will happen if you train hard for a few months and then quit? Will you lose everything you've worked hard to gain? No. If you suddenly quit after training for a period of time, you will lose a little of what you gained, but your speed will not return back to its original level unless you take a lengthy (more than six months) layoff. And even if you do this, it will return to the level you built it to in just a few weeks after resuming training. So even if you are planning to take a few weeks off now and then, it won't hurt your progress for long.

Do you have to be an Olympic sprinter or an exceptional athlete to use and benefit from these programs? Absolutely not. As a matter of fact, these programs were designed primarily to help the mediocre athlete become faster so that he could compete on a more even keel with the "natural" athlete. This is not to deny the effectiveness that these programs can have for athletes who have already exhibited superior abilities. Their use of the outlined plans may make them even more successful. So regardless if you are already very fast or you lumber like an ox, or whether you want more speed to run for touchdowns or just to rush to the net in tennis, the programs outlined in this book can be used to your advantage.

Finally, **what kind of specific results can you expect?** Or how much time will these programs actually cut off your running times and add to your quickness? I wish I could answer that, but there are so many variables involved that any answer that I could give you would be pure speculation. The best that I can do is to tell you about the kinds of results other athletes are getting with use of these types of programs. So here goes.

As a rule, most athletes reduce their forty-yard running time by .2 to .4 of a second, their 100-yard running time by .6 to one full second, and add greatly to their explosiveness off the mark with about six months of consistent training. Again these are just averages. You may do better than this or you may not do quite as well. That is not meant to discourage you — just to let you know that there are no guarantees. The bottom line comes down to what you put into it. If you take the attitude that you won't be denied and you train hard and consistently, you will gain speed. And who knows? Someday you may surprise the world just the way Borzov did in 1972. Good luck.

Index